Specialities of Tyrolean cooking

Selected and Compiled
by
Lotte Scheibenpflug

Pinguin-Verlag, Innsbruck

The colour illustrations were produce from photographs
specially taken for this book by Ferdinand Schreiber of Salzburg
Drawings: Dr. Brinna Otto
English translation: Jacqueline Schweighofer

© 1986 by Pinguin-Verlag
A-6021 Innsbruck
All rights reserved
Printed by Carl Ueberreuter Druckerei Ges. m. b. H.,
2100 Korneuburg
Lithography: Ifolith, Innsbruck
Printed in Austria
ISBN 3-7016-2222-1

Contents

Meat and Fish

Deep-Fried Batters

Puddings, Cakes and Pastries

Tyrolean Cooking

In its basic elements Tyrolean cooking corresponds – or rather, corresponded – to the natural conditions and the agricultural utilization of this region. Everything that thrived in the mild climate on the southern side of the Alps and everything that the mountain farmers wrested from the meagre and steep slopes in the north of the province was placed on the table in the form of traditional, local dishes. That explains why Tyrolean cooking emphasized food prepared from various cereals, wild berries, fruit from the garden, home-grown vegetables and meat – this usually being reserved for high days and holidays – obtained from one's own stocks or brought home from the hunt.

In the course of recent decades the valleys have been opened up to tourism and a wealth of produce from all over the world is now available in even the tiniest places. This has decisively altered Tyrolean cooking and Tyrolean eating habits. Many of the typical old dishes are no longer prepared, having disappeared from the kitchens of private households and inns alike. Memories of the art of cooking as practised by previous generations have stimulated an interest in local dishes, however, and in the Tyrol both north and south of the Brenner there are earnest endeavours to revive these dishes. Hand in hand with this, we observe attempts to provide "natural cooking", a cuisine which makes use of the natural produce once customary and which aims at healthier nutrition.

This book presents a modest selection of traditional Tyrolean dishes, dishes well worth preparing at home now and again. The ingredients are readily available and the recipes are not difficult to follow. All have been tried and tested. We hope that readers will enjoy both preparing and eating them.

Soups

Tiroler Backerbsensuppe
Soup with Batter Morsels

Ingredients:
1 egg
1 egg white
pinch of salt
1 dessertspoon oil
flour as required
fat for frying

Method:
Mix all ingredients to a smooth batter. Heat some lard until very hot. Holding a grater upside down, drip batter through this into the hot fat, making sure that the pan is not too full. Remove each batch of pea-sized batter morsels as soon as these have turned golden brown.

Drain well and serve separately with consommé of beef.

Fleischkrapfl-Suppe
Soup with Miniature Meat Pasties

Ingredients:
2 l. beef consommé
150 g. meat left-overs
100 g. flour
1 dessertspoon oil
20 g. butter
1 egg
2 dessertspoons water
1 finely chopped onion
1 dessertspoon chopped herbs

Method:
Mix the flour, 1 egg yolk, water, salt and oil to a dough. Fry onion and herbs in the hot butter, add meat and cook well. Roll out dough thinly, place small mounds of meat filling on top, each about 3 fingers apart, brush with white of egg and fold into triangles. Cook in boiling soup for about 5 to 7 minutes.

These miniature pasties can also be brushed with egg and baked in the oven before being served with the soup.

Vinschgauer Suppe
Vinschgau Soup

Ingredients:
1 l. water
300 g. beef
250 g. root vegetables (e.g. carrots, celeriac, leeks)
pinch of salt
pepper
1 clove of garlic
1 slice of brown bread per person

Method:
Clean and chop vegetables and cook together with meat and seasonings for $1\frac{1}{2}$ hours, then remove from liquid and dice. The bread should also be diced and placed in the soup with the meat before serving.

Tiroler Brotsuppe
Tyrolean Bread Soup

Ingredients:
150 g. dry brown bread
40 g. fat
1 small onion
1 l. consommé (or water)
pinch of salt
nutmeg
1 dessertspoon chives
1 or 2 eggs

Method:
Fry the finely chopped onion in the fat, add the bread, cut into small pieces, let the mixture cook a little, then add a little liquid and cook for approx. 15 minutes. Add the remaining liquid, let the mixture boil up again, season and, if desired, whisk the egg or eggs into the soup.
The onion can also be fried with finely chopped bacon and diced sausages can be added to the soup before serving.

Tiroler Schöberlsuppe
Soup with Sponge Fingers

The *Schöberl* is a sort of unsweetened sponge cake, baked in a flat tin and cut into fingers to be served in soup. There are many different flavourings (peas, parmesan cheese etc.), but bacon is the typical ingredient of the *Tiroler Schöberl.*

Ingredients:
2 eggs
40 g. flour
pinch of salt
80 g. Tyrolean bacon (or smoked meat)
a little butter and flour for the tin

Method:
Cream the butter and egg yolks, add the flour and the finely diced bacon, season with salt and fold in the stiffly beaten egg whites. Grease a square tin with the butter, dust with flour, pour in the mixture and bake in a hot oven (220° C) for about 12 minutes. Turn out immediately and cut into squares or diamonds. Pour consommé over the fingers just before serving.

Brennsuppe
Brown Soup

This simplest and cheapest of soups was known everywhere throughout the peasant world. A meal for "poor people", it was frequently the only hot food they got and it was often eaten for breakfast. This soup still features in farming life today during the Lenten period.

Ingredients:
50–60 g. dark flour
40 g. butter or dripping
1 l. clear soup or simply water
pinch of salt
caraway
lovage

Method:
Fry the flour in the hot fat until it is lightly browned, then gradually add the water or soup, stirring well to prevent lumps. Whisk, season and cook gently for at least half an hour until the soup thickens. It is served with croûtons, but sliced, boiled potatoes can also be added to this soup.

Cereals
and
Starch Foods

Tiroler Speckknödel
Tyrolean Bacon Dumplings

One of the main features of Tyrolean cookery, these have almost become a symbol. There may be many secret recipes for them, but in fact they are simply bread dumplings to which bacon, sausage or smoked meat are added. These bacon dumplings thus vary from house to house, according to what is added and on account of the different seasonings. This recipe is one of many, but provides a standard example of traditional Tyrolean fare.

Ingredients:
300 g. stale rolls
100 to 150 g. bacon (or bacon and cold sausage)
2 eggs
approx. 2 dessertspoons flour
$\frac{1}{8}$ l. milk
1 small onion
1 dessertspoon butter
2 dessertspoons chopped parsley
pinch of salt
marjoram
1 dessertspoon chopped chives
small pinch of ground pepper

Method:
Fry the chopped onion in butter and mix with the diced bread and chopped bacon (and sausage, if desired). Whisk the eggs with the milk and pour over the bread and bacon mixture. Leave to stand for about 15 minutes, then stir in the parsley, chives and flour and add the remaining seasonings (these can be

varied according to taste). Moistening the hands, shape the mixture into dumplings (approx. 8), adding flour if necessary. Cook in boiling, salted water for 10–15 minutes.

Leberknödel
Liver Dumplings

Ingredients:
2 stale rolls
50 g. butter
1 small onion
100 g. liver (beef or pig's)
50 g. milt (if this is not available, another 50 g. liver)
1 egg
$\frac{1}{8}$ l. milk
1 dessertspoon chopped parsley
pinch of salt
pinch of pepper
$\frac{1}{2}$ teaspoon marjoram
garlic
breadcrumbs as required

Method:
Leave the bread to soak for a while in the hot milk. Meanwhile, fry the finely chopped onion in the butter, mix with the finely minced liver and milt, parsley and seasonings, stir in the egg and blend with the bread from which the liquid should be pressed out. Shape the mixture into dumplings, adding breadcrumbs as required for easier handling. Bring dumplings to the boil in salted water and leave at a gentle boil for about 12 minutes. These dumplings are either served in consommé or are eaten as a main course, preferably with sauerkraut.

Tiroler Grießknödel
Semolina Dumplings

Ingredients:
200 g. semolina (not too fine)
2 eggs
¼ l. milk
1 stale roll (or several slices of bread)
1 dessertspoon chopped parsley
50 g. Tyrolean bacon
pinch of salt
nutmeg

Method:
Boil the semolina in the milk, to which the butter has been added, add salt and stir until the mixture leaves the side of the pan. Allow to cool a little. Dice the bacon and fry with the diced roll or bread. Beat the two eggs and blend well with the fried bread, chopped parsley, nutmeg and semolina mixture. Moistening the hands, shape the mixture into dumplings and cook these in boiling salted water for 10–15 minutes.

These semolina dumplings are served with sauerkraut, but they go well with game dishes or roast pork, too. They can also be served in soup.

Wasserspatzln
Tyrolean-Style Pasta

Ingredients:
300 g. flour
2 eggs
pinch of salt
approx. ¼ l. water

Method:
Mix all the ingredients to a firm dough and press these through a large-hole strainer into an ample amount of boiling salted water. Cook slowly, cool down with cold water. These Spatzln are frequently served to accompany meat or, mixed with sausage, bacon or eggs, as a main dish with salad.

Käsespatzln
Cheese Pasta

Ingredients:
Wasserspatzln (as described in previous recipe)
50 g. butter
100 g. grated cheese
pinch of salt
1 dessertspoon parsley
1 small onion

Method:
Chop the onion finely, fry in the butter, add the cooked pasta and chopped parsley, sprinkle with grated cheese and serve with a green salad.

Right: Vinschgau Soup (recipe page 13); left: Polenta Slices (recipe page 38), behind: Meran-Style Chocolate Sponge Roll (recipe page 77).

Tyrolean Bacon Dumplings (recipe page 19).

Schlickkrapferln

These are made of noodle dough, which is why they are also known as "cheese noodles" or "stuffed noodles". In the valleys of the East Tyrol they were, and still are, a traditionally popular dish, the preparation of which varies greatly from place to place and from farm to farm. It usually depends on what ingredients happen to be available. Basically, the principle is to cut out squares or circles of noodle dough and to fill these with spinach, cheese, cream cheese, herbs or a mixture of several of these ingredients and then to cook them in salted water.

Ingredients:
For the dough:

500 g. flour	or: 300 g. wheat flour and
1 to 2 eggs	200 g. rye flour
1 dessertspoon oil	2 dessertspoons oil
pinch of salt	pinch of salt
water as required	water as required

For the filling:
300 g. cream cheese (dry, pressed)
300 g. spinach (cooked and finely chopped)
200 g. coarse breadcrumbs
1 small onion, chopped
pinch of salt
1 dessertspoon each of chopped parsley and chives
nutmeg
pepper
1 dessertspoon grated cheese (if desired)

Method:
Knead the dough ingredients well in a bowl, allow to rest for about one hour. Roll out thinly, cut into

squares or into circles with a glass. Mix the ingredients for the filling, place little mounds of the mixture on the paste shapes, fold over and press edges down well.

The *Schlickkrapferln* are cooked in boiling salted water (approx. 7–10 minutes) and served with melted butter or with fried bacon.

Schlutzkrapfen

The South Tyrolean version of the East Tyrolean *Schlickkrapferln*. These are also made of noodle dough, but strudel pastry can be used, too (see page 79). The *Schlutzkrapfen* are either filled with well seasoned spinach which has been passed through a sieve or with a mixture of fried bread, cream cheese and herbs. Preparation as for *Schlickkrapferln*.

Kasnudeln
Cheese Noodles

By "noodles" one usually means pasta, made of flour, egg and water, cooked in various forms (usually ribbon-shaped) and either served to accompany meat dishes or eaten as a main dish with cheese, bacon, meat, ham, breadcrumbs or cabbage. Today, home-made noodles are a somewhat rare speciality, prepared in private homes for festive occasions.

Ingredients for the noodle pasta:
300 g. flour
2 eggs
1 dessertspoon oil
pinch of salt
approx. 5 dessertspoons water

Method:
Put the flour in a mound on a suitable surface (marble slab, wooden pastry board etc.), make a well in the centre and add the eggs. Add salt and oil. Add water, mixing well and kneading to a firm, elastic dough. Leave to rest for half an hour, then roll out thinner and thinner with a long rolling pin. Dry this piece of dough (not letting it get hard) and cut it into strips on a floured board.
Cook the noodles in ample boiling water (approx. 1 l. water and 1 teaspoon salt to 100 g noodles), cool with cold water, dry in the air again and then prepare further, as required.

Cheese noodles

These are made from home-made or bought ribbon-shaped noodles which are drained, turned in butter in a pan and mixed either with crumbled Tyrolean *Graukäse* or with ample grated cheese. They served with melted butter and, if desired, with fried onions.

Erdäpfelnudeln
Potato Noodles

Ingredients:
750 g. potatoes
200 g. flour
1 egg
pinch of salt
nutmeg

Method:
Boil the potatoes without peeling, then peel, pass through a sieve or food mill and mix with the egg, flour and seasoning. Since the firmness of the dough depends on the variety of potato, it might be necessary to add more flour. Shape the dough into cylindrical noodles, the size of a little finger, drop them into boiling salted water and boil gently until they rise to the top. Remove with a draining spoon.
Potato noodles can be served with game dishes and roast meat in gravy or they can be prepared with breadcrumbs browned in butter, or with butter and grated cheese, or with sugar and ground poppy seed.

Tiroler Bauernmus
Tyrolean Gruel

Even in the post-war period this gruel was practically the staple diet of the farming community. If there was hard work to be done, the *Mus* was eaten for breakfast, otherwise it was frequently a supper dish.

Ingredients:
250 g. flour (or 125 g. flour and 125 g. semolina)
50 g. butter
1 l. milk
1 l. water
1 teaspoon salt
30 g. butter or clarified butter to grease the pan

Method:
Grease a large pan (preferably cast iron) with the fat, then boil the milk and water in this. Stir in the flour (or flour and semolina mixture). The flour can be mixed with a little cold water first to prevent lumps forming. Lowering the heat, let the gruel thicken. Before serving, remove from the heat and leave covered for a short while so that the surface becomes firm. Distribute the butter over the gruel in small pieces or pour melted butter over it.

In some areas the *Mus* is prepared with oatmeal. If maize flour is used instead of flour, the dish is known as "Turkish Gruel" (see polenta).

Semmelschmarrn
Bread Pancakes

Ingredients:
5–6 rolls baked the previous day
½ l. milk
2 eggs
80 g. butter
pinch of salt
80 g. sugar
Further, if desired:
30 g. raisins or sultanas
30 g. almonds
cinnamon
lemon peel

Method:
Cut the rolls into thin slices and pour over the milk which has been whisked with the eggs, salt and a little butter. Leave to stand for a while, then heat the butter in a wide pan, add the bread mixture and fry the *Schmarrn* quickly and thoroughly, adding the raisins and spices, if desired. Sprinkle with sugar and serve hot.

There is also a savoury variation, chopped bacon (or smoked meat or cold roast meat) being added to the bread, milk and egg mixture and the dish being served with salad or with sauerkraut.

Kaiserschmarrn
Chopped Pancake

Ingredients:
150 g. flour
3 eggs
60 g. butter
pinch of salt
approx. ¼ l. milk
1 dessertspoon sugar
40 g. raisins or sultanas

Method:
Mix the flour, milk, salt and egg yolks well. Add the stiffly beaten whites of the three eggs. Heat half the butter in a thick pan, pour in the batter, add the soaked and drained raisins. Fry well, then lift the pancake, add the rest of the butter to the pan and fry the pancake on the other side, too. Cut into small pieces with two forks, sprinkle with icing sugar and serve. In the Tyrol this is served with cranberries or with cooked damsons. (The custom of serving it with stewed, frequently tinned, fruit – or even with pine-apple slices – has unfortunately become common in the age of mass tourism!)

„Kaiserschmarrn" (recipe page 34) and, behind, Apple Fritters (recipe page 71).

Tyrolean-Style Bread and Butter Pudding (recipe page 75).

Moosbeernocken
Bilberry Pancakes

Also known as *Schwarzbeernocken* or *Blaubeernocken,* these pancakes are always prepared with bilberries (blueberries). They are a traditionally popular dish throughout the whole of the Tyrol, although the method of preparation varies greatly. In fact, these pancakes are a variation of *Kaiserschmarrn* and are simple to make.

Ingredients:
3 whole eggs
150 g. flour
200 g. bilberries
50 g. butter
pinch of salt
$\frac{1}{8}$ l. milk

Method:
Mix the milk, flour, eggs and salt. Add the well drained berries to the mixture. Heat the butter in a pan and put spoonfuls of the mixture, about the size of the palm of the hand, into the hot fat, ensuring that there is enough room for each pancake to spread out. Fry on both sides and serve with sugar or with sugar and cinnamon.

Polenta

A porridge made from yellow maize flour, polenta is one of the staple foods of northern Italy. In the Tyrol it became known as *Plenten* and here – particularly in the South Tyrol – this dish is either made of maize flour or of buckwheat, when it is called *Schwarzplenten*.

Ingredients:
300 g. polenta (fine)
1 l. water
1 teaspoon salt

Method:
Using a wooden spoon, carefully stir the polenta into the fast boiling water and cook for approx. 25–30 minutes, stirring continuously. The polenta then leaves the sides of the pan easily and can be smoothed into a dish or simply turned out on to a moistened surface.
It can either be cut into slices and eaten at once with various meat dishes (ragout of game, goulash etc.) or with browned butter and parmesan cheese, or it can be left until cold, cut into slices and fried in butter. In this case it is served with meat or stewed fruit, sugar being added to the polenta in the latter case.

Schwarzplenten
Buckwheat Porridge

Like polenta, buckwheat porridge was a popular dish in various parts of the Tyrol, either for breakfast or to accompany various dishes. Buckwheat was once cultivated in the east and the south Tyrol and was called *Schwarzplenten,* or "black polenta", to distinguish it from the yellow maize flour.

Ingredients:
Use 1 cup of water for every 30 g. buckwheat. Milk, or a mixture of water and milk, can also be used.
pinch of salt
50 g. butter or bacon

Method:
Stir the buckwheat together with the lukewarm water, add salt and put aside to soak. Then heat the butter (or fry the bacon) and cook the buckwheat in this fat, turning frequently.
If preferred, the buckwheat can be boiled first in the water, then left to soak for 20–30 minutes before being served either with hot butter, fried bacon, onions and parsley, or with butter, sugar and milk.

Riebler

Made of semolina or of maize semolina which is boiled in milk and then fried, the *Riebel* is a traditional dish in many parts of the Tyrol. It is served in many different ways–with bacon and onions or with sugar, jam, cinnamon and stewed fruit–and is typical of the simple, traditional meals prepared from home produce. The end product can be somewhat dry, unless served with plenty of fried bacon, melted butter or dripping, and that is why it is frequently known as "stick-in-the-throat"!

Maize Riebler

Ingredients:
150 g. maize semolina
½ l. milk
50 g. butter
pinch of salt
butter for frying

Method:
Boil up the milk, add the salt and butter, pour in the maize semolina, stirring constantly, and continue to cook until the porridge leaves the side of the saucepan. Heat the butter in a pan and add spoonfuls of the mixture, dividing into small pieces with two forks and frying well. This frequently provides a hearty breakfast dish or it is served with meat, sauerkraut or salad. If sugar is sprinkled over it, it can also be served with stewed fruit.

Turkish Riebler

Ingredients:
250 g. maize semolina
¼ l. water
pinch of salt

Method:
Pour the boiling salted water over the maize semolina and leave to soak for at least one hour. Then fry the mixture in plenty of hot butter in a pan. Thin slices of apple can also be added to this dish.

Meat and Fish

Tyrolean-Style Saddle of Chamois (recipe page 58).

Tyrolean Liver (recipe page 54), Tyrolean Bubble and Squeak at back (recipe page 47) and Tyrolean Bacon Dumplings at top (recipe page 19).

Tiroler Gröstl
Tyrolean Bubble and Squeak

The ingredients of this dish rather depend on what is left over from the day before and what is available in the house. Potatoes always form the basis of a Gröstl, however. For a truly authentic Tiroler Gröstl some pork is required:

Ingredients:
400 g. pork (left-overs from a roast joint etc.)
600 g. cooked potatoes
1 large onion
80 g. butter
salt
pepper
caraway
marjoram
parsley

Method:
Fry the finely chopped onion in a little butter, add the diced meat, season, add the finely sliced potatoes and the remaining butter and fry well. Sprinkle with chopped parsley before serving.
If the only left-overs available are of beef, the dish is known as Bauerngröstl, or farmer's bubble and squeak. Slices of sausage, ham or other meat can be used instead of the pork. If veal pieces, more fat and less potatoes are used, the dish is called Herrengröstl (lord's bubble and squeak). This can also be served with one fried egg per person.

Tiroler Kalbsstelze
Tyrolean Knuckle of Veal

Ingredients:
One knuckle is sufficient for 2 people
4 dessertspoons butter
1 finely chopped clove of garlic
a pinch of salt and a little pepper are also required

Method:
Wash the meat and rub in the salt, pepper and garlic.
Melt the butter in a frying pan and fry the meat until
golden brown all over, basting continuously. Pour a
dessertspoon of water over the meat from time to
time. Test whether the meat is cooked by pricking
with a fork: the liquid emerging should be quite
clear. Arrange on a heated serving dish and serve
with rice or potatoes and a mixed salad.

Tiroler Rindsbraten
Tyrolean Braised Beef

Ingredients:
1 kg. beef (a cut suitable for braising)
50 g. oil
80 g. Tyrolean bacon
$\frac{1}{8}$ l. red wine
1 carrot
1 root of parsley
$\frac{1}{2}$ celeriac root
1 leek
1 onion
1–2 cloves of garlic
1 dessertspoon flour
$\frac{1}{2}$ l. clear soup
1 dessertspoon tomato puree
pinch of salt
pepper
$\frac{1}{2}$ teaspoon each of caraway and marjoram
500 g. potatoes

Method:
Cut the bacon into thin strips and lard the meat with this. Chop the onion finely, press out the garlic, sauté both in the oil and then add the meat and fry well on each side. Wash and chop the vegetables, add to the meat, season, add the soup and the wine and braise slowly. Add the peeled and diced potatoes for the last half hour of cooking time. Serve with slices of polenta or with pasta.

Schweinsbraten auf Bauernart
Country-Style Roast Pork

Ingredients:
1 kg. pork (a cut suitable for roasting, e. g. shoulder, loin or leg)
1 dessertspoon butter
1 cup of soup
1 clove of garlic
pinch of salt
pepper
1 teaspoon caraway
1 teaspoon thyme

Method:
Rub the joint of meat well with the seasonings, brush with butter and cook in a heavy roasting pan in a pre-heated oven for approx. $1\frac{1}{2}$–2 hours, basting frequently with the juices from the meat and with the soup.
In the Tyrol roast pork is usually served with bread dumplings and a green salad. Sauerkraut and potatoes – these can be roasted with the meat, if desired – are also suitable accompaniments.

Krenfleisch
Roast Pork with Horseradish

Ingredients:
600–800 g. belly of pork
1 onion
1 bay leaf
⅛ l. vinegar
pinch of salt
peppercorns
root vegetables (3 carrots, ½ celeriac root, 1–2 roots of parsley)
⅛ l. vinegar
a piece of horseradish (approx. 150 g.) or a jar of grated horseradish

Method:
Bring the vegetables, seasonings and vinegar to the boil with approx. ½ l water. The meat should be cut into slices, these having the thickness of a finger, and should be boiled in the above mixture for approx. 30 minutes. The peeled, diced potatoes are then added and the whole mixture is steamed until tender. Serve the meat together with the vegetables and potatoes, sprinkling the grated horseradish in a thick layer over the top.

Bröselfleisch
Beef with Breadcrumbs

An hors-d'œvre frequently served at festive meals (weddings etc.) in the Tyrol. It is often eaten as a simple supper dish, too.

Ingredients:
Beef cooked as soup (approx. 100 g. per person)
breadcrumbs fried in butter (2 dessertspoons per person)
chopped onion sautéd in fat (1 dessertspoon per person)

Method:
Cut the meat into thin slices whilst still warm and arrange with the fried breadcrumbs and onions.
If this constitutes a whole meal, serve with green salad or potato salad.

Tiroler Gulasch
Tyrolean Goulash

Ingredients:
600 g. stewing beef
60 g. butter
150 g. Tyrolean bacon
400 g. onions
1 dessertspoon paprika
1 dessertspoon caraway seed
1 dessertspoon marjoram
pinch of pepper
pinch of salt
1 clove of garlic
piece of lemon peel
approx. $\frac{1}{8}$ l. water or consommé

Method:
Dice the bacon and fry in the butter, adding the chopped onion and the paprika. Then add the cubes of meat and some water or consommé. Cover and cook slowly, adding the remaining seasonings and some more liquid from time to time. Continue to cook until the meat is tender and the onions are completely incorporated in the liquid. The resulting gravy should have a creamy consistency. If desired, a few pieces of dry brown bread can be added and cooked with the meat. In the Tyrol polenta or dumplings are usually served with goulash, but boiled potatoes are also a suitable accompaniment.

Tiroler Leber
Tyrolean Liver

Ingredients:
4 slices of calf's liver (each weighing approx. 120 g.)
60 g. Tyrolean bacon
50 g. butter
pinch of salt
pepper
1 dessertspoon flour
$\frac{1}{8}$ l. soup

Method:
Fry the bacon in the butter, add the slices of liver and fry quickly on each side. Cooking too long makes the liver hard. Dust with the flour, season with the pepper and add the soup, steam for a little longer and then add the salt. Serve at once. Boiled potatoes and a green salad are suitable accompaniments.

Tyrolean Knuckle of Veal (recipe page 48) with snowy Kössen in the Kaiser range as a background.

Tyrolean Fritters with „Nuischmalz" in front of the Ötztal mountain panorama (recipe page 69).

Hirschrücken "Unterland"
Saddle of Venison

Ingredients:
1 whole saddle of venison
100 g. bacon
salt
pepper
oil
a bunch of parsley
50 g. bacon
100 g. chanterelles or mushrooms

Method:
The venison should be well hung before cooking.
Rub each side with salt, pepper and oil, lard with
bacon and roast in the oven. Fry small rashers of
bacon, add the parsley and garnish the venison with
this and with the cooked mushrooms. Serve with polenta (Page 38) and cranberries.

Gemsrücken nach Tiroler Art
Tyrolean-Style Saddle of Chamois

Lard the chamois and marinate for 3 to 4 days in the marinade described below. Remove, dry, season with salt and pepper and roast, basting with a sauce made from the marinade whisked with $\frac{1}{4}$ l. sour cream. There should be sufficient liquid for the chamois to be braised in the oven rather than roast.

Sauce to serve with the prepared roast chamois: 2 to 3 slices of brown bread, 1 thick slice of hard gingerbread, 2 dessertspoons rosehip jam, a little lemon juice, 1 glass red wine. Cook these ingredients into a sauce, carve the meat before serving and pour the sauce over the top.
Serve with cranberry sauce, chestnuts, bread dumplings or polenta.

Recipe for cooked chestnuts: Score the chestnuts across, cook them and remove the shell and the skin whilst still hot. Then simmer them with a little butter, sugar, salt, ground nutmeg and milk until they are soft.

Marinade for the saddle of chamois: Quantities for a whole saddle (2 to $2\frac{1}{2}$ kg. meat): $\frac{1}{2}$ l. water, $\frac{1}{16}$ l. vinegar, 100 g. chopped vegetables, a thinly sliced onion, a few peppercorns and coriander seeds, 1 bay leaf, some thyme, a few juniper berries, 1 wedge of lemon. Boil together for 15 minutes. Do not use salt or the meat will turn red.
Allow the marinade to become quite cold before pouring over the meat. When the meat is removed from the marinade, do not discard this as it is required for basting (see above).

Hendl in Rahmsoße
Chicken in Cream Sauce

Ingredients:
1 roasting chicken
1 large onion
$\frac{1}{8}$ l. white wine
60 g. butter
$\frac{1}{2}$ teaspoon rosemary
salt
pepper
$\frac{1}{4}$ l sour cream
1 cup of chicken soup
1 dessertspoon flour

Method:
Joint the chicken into 8 pieces. Finely chop the onion, sauté in the hot butter, add the chicken pieces and fry on all sides. Add the white wine, salt, pepper and rosemary, fry well, then add the soup and steam until tender. Mix the flour with the sour cream and pour this over the chicken when it is cooked. Serve with slices of polenta or with rice.

Jungente, Tiroler Art
Tyrolean-Style Duckling

Ingredients:
1 duckling
50 g. butter
150 g. Tyrolean bacon
1 large onion
$\frac{1}{8}$ l. red wine
2 dessertspoons cranberries
2 dessertspoons sour cream
pinch of salt
pepper
marjoram
mugwort
1 dessertspoon flour

Method:
Remove the entrails, clean the duckling well inside and out, dry and then rub the inside with salt, marjoram and mugwort. Cut the bacon up small and fry in a pan together with the chopped onion. Place the duckling in the pan, breast downwards, brush with butter and roast in the oven until crisp, turning once. Then remove the duck and keep hot, pour off the surplus fat, add the red wine to the remaining fat, bind with flour and sour cream and allow it to thicken a little. Stir in the cranberries, pour this sauce over the carved duckling and serve. In the Tyrol this dish is eaten with bread dumplings, potato noodles or roast potatoes and warm cabbage salad (with cooked bacon and caraway seed).

Forelle blau
Poached Trout

Ingredients:
4 trout
For the court-bouillon:
2 dessertspoons vinegar
2 dessertspoons white wine
1 onion cut in rings
several black peppercorns
several pimento (allspice) berries
1 bay leaf
80 g. butter
parsley and lemon to garnish

Method:
Clean out the fresh trout and wash carefully in cold water without damaging the scales. Using a fish kettle or a flat saucepan, bring some lightly salted water to the boil with the court-bouillon. Add the trout, turning down the heat so that they are lightly poached and leaving them until the eyes bulge and the scales can be removed easily (8–10 minutes). Serve on a heated dish with parsley and slices of lemon, together with boiled potatoes and the melted butter.

Forelle gebraten
Fried trout

Ingredients:
4 trout
3 dessertspoons flour
1 dessertspoon lemon juice
1 teaspoon salt
100 g. butter
parsley and slices of lemon to garnish

Method:
Carefully clean out the fresh trout and wash in cold
water, pat dry, salt the inside, sprinkle with lemon
juice, dust with flour and fry in butter until brown on
both sides. Serve at once on a heated dish and garnish with the lemon and parsley. Parsley potatoes
and a green salad are served with this dish.

Deep-Fried Batters

Tirteln

A traditionally popular dish in the South and the East Tyrol. Basically, it is made of simple noodle dough, rolled out into thin slices. Two of these slices are filled with mixtures of cream cheese or vegetables and are shaped into a pasty which is then fried in deep fat. The *Tirteln* are served hot, usually accompanied by a green salad.

Ingredients:
Dough:
300 g. flour (wheat or rye or a mixture of both)
pinch of salt
lukewarm water as required
Filling:
Well-seasoned, cooked, thickened spinach or sauerkraut, cut up small and fried in bacon or a mixture of cream cheese and herbs

Method:
Prepare a noodle dough with the flour and water, kneading it thoroughly and then leaving it to rest. Cut pieces off this dough, roll them out and shape into circles (10–15 cm. in diameter). Place a teaspoon of the filling on half of the batch and cover with the remaining circles, pressing down the edges well. The resulting pasties should be fried golden brown in clarified butter or in oil before being drained and served hot.

Strauben

This dish plays an important part in traditional Tyrolean cooking, primarily being prepared on feast-days. When the sugar was omitted, this was also a popular main meal, served with milk, coffee or stewed fruit. Various batters are used for *Strauben,* but milk or cream are always among the ingredients, as are eggs. Strauben batter should always be very smooth and liquid. It is poured into the hot cooking fat (usually clarified butter) with the aid of a special spoon or funnel, although any vessel with a lip or a normal funnel will also do. Squiggles, spirals or other shapes can be made. Two examples of batter recipes:

Ingredients:
200 g. flour
2 eggs
¼ l. milk
pinch of salt
2 dessertspoons rum (or an eau-de-vie made from fruit)
cooking fat

Method:
Stir the flour gradually into the lukewarm milk (a little butter or cream can also be added), mix in the egg yolks, stir in the rum or eau-de-vie and then fold in the stiffly beaten egg whites. Drop the smooth, flowing batter into the hot fat and fry until golden brown.

Strauben made of choux pastry

Ingredients:
150 g. flour
70 g. butter
¼ l. milk (or water)
pinch of salt
4 eggs
2 dessertspoons rum

Method:
Bring the milk (water), salt and butter to the boil, add all the flour at once and mix well until the mixture is quite smooth and starts to leave the sides of the pan. Beat in the eggs, add the rum and beat thoroughly until the mixture is smooth and shiny and can be dropped into the hot fat.

Tiroler Kirchtagskrapfen
Tyrolean Fritters

Once traditional fare at church festivals and parish fairs, these fritters have all different sorts of fillings, depending on the area in which they are made. The composition of the dough–it is more of a dough than a batter–also varies greatly from place to place. Basically, it is a kind of fine noodle dough; after being left to rest, it is divided into two strips, the filling being placed on one strip and covered with the other. The fritters are then cut out and fried in hot fat on both sides.

Ingredients:
250 g. flour
40 g. butter
1 egg
1 dessertspoon rum
approx. ⅛ l. lukewarm milk

Method:
Mix a dough with the salted flour, the melted butter, the egg and the milk; knead well. Divide into two halves and roll both out very thinly. Distribute the filling at regular intervals over one half of the pastry and cover with the second strip. Press down well between the spoonfuls of filling and cut out squares. Fry on both sides in plenty of fat.

Filling:
This can consist of finely chopped prunes, dried pears (previously cooked), raisins, sugar, cinnamon and cloves and a little schnaps or eau-de-vie. The mixture should be cooked with butter and milk until it thickens and must be allowed to cool before use.

Cranberries mixed with breadcrumbs can also be used, so can a filling of poppy seed with sugar and raisins. Today these fritters frequently just have a simple jam filling.

Here a recipe for a special kind of *Kirchtagskrapfen:*

Kirchtagskrapfen aus dem Ötztal mit Nuischmalz
Ötztal Fritters with Nuischmalz

Ingredients:
45 g. butter
500 g. flour
1 egg
pinch of salt
lukewarm water as required

Method:
Work ingredients into a firm dough, leave to rest for ½ hour, roll out thinly until almost transparent. Cut into squares, place filling on one and cover with another, press down firmly and deep fry in hot lard.

Filling:
½ l. milk
1 dessertspoon sugar
650 g. butter
flour as required
Soak 200 g. dried pears, 200 g. figs and 200 g. prunes overnight, chop into small pieces and bind with 200 g. ground poppy seed, 100 g. breadcrumbs and 1 dessertspoon rum.
These special fritters are traditionally served with *Nuischmalz* ("new dripping") which is prepared in

the following way: Pour $\frac{1}{2}$ l. milk into a large pan and warm it over medium heat. Add sufficient flour to form a thick porridge and let this come to the boil, stirring continuously. Add 1 dessertspoon sugar and allow to cool slowly, again stirring all the time. As soon as the mixture is lukewarm, stir in 650 g. butter and allow to cool completely, stirring constantly. Altogether at least $\frac{1}{2}$ hour must be allowed for stirring.

Once the mixture has become stiff, pile it up in a pyramid on a plate using a spoon or spatula, and pour liquid honey over the top.

Apfelradeln (Apfelkiachln)
Apple Fritters

Ingredients:
$\frac{1}{8}$ l. milk
100 g. flour
salt
1 egg
10 g. sugar
$\frac{1}{2}$ dessertspoon rum
6–8 medium-sized apples
fat for frying

Method:
Mix the flour, salt and milk and add the egg, sugar and rum, beating to obtain a thick batter. Peel and core the apples, cut into slices $\frac{1}{2}$ cm. thick, dip these into the batter and fry in the hot butter. Drain on greaseproof paper, sprinkle with cinnamon and sugar and serve hot.

In the Tyrol apple fritters are frequently made with a wine batter

Ingredients for wine batter:
100 g. flour
$\frac{1}{8}$ l. white wine
pinch of salt
1 dessertspoon icing sugar
1 egg
fat for frying

Puddings, Cakes and Pastries

Scheiterhaufen
Tyrolean-Style Bread and Butter Pudding

Ingredients:
6 stale rolls (or stale white bread or croissants)
⅜ l. milk
2 eggs
½ kg. apples
30 g. raisins
30 g. almonds
80 g. butter
80 g. sugar

Method:
Slice the rolls thinly, whisk the eggs, sugar, milk and half of the butter und pour this mixture over the bread. Peel and core the apples, cut into thin slices and mix with the raisins and almond slivers. Grease a fireproof dish and place layers of the bread mixture and the apples in this dish, finishing with a layer of the bread mixture. Dot with the remaining butter. Bake for 30–40 minutes in a moderate oven until the pudding is golden brown. Serve hot.

Tiroler Bröselkuchen
Tyrolean Breadcrumb Cake

Ingredients:
5 eggs
the weight of five eggs in sugar
the weight of five eggs in breadcrumbs (at least half
of these should be brown breadcrumbs)
1 teaspoon cinnamon
1 teaspoon pimento (allspice, mixed spice)
1 teaspoon baking powder
pinch of salt

Method:
Beat the egg yolks and the sugar until light, add the
breadcrumbs, salt, baking powder and spices, fold in
the stiffly beaten eggs whites. Pour the mixture into
an oblong tin and bake in a hot oven (220° C) for approx. 25 minutes.
Cut the cake into thick slices whilst still hot and serve
with hot mulled wine (boil up red wine with sugar,
cinnamon and cloves). Pour the mulled wine over the
cake at table.

Schokoladeroulade "Meran"
Meran-Style Chocolate Sponge Roll

Ingredients:
1 egg yolk
1 dessertspoon sugar
1 dessertspoon cocoa or drinking chocolate
2 egg whites
$\frac{1}{4}$ l. cream

Method:
Beat the egg yolks and the sugar until light, stir in the cocoa and carefully fold in the stiffly beaten egg whites. Spread the mixture over a greased baking tray so that it has the thickness of a finger and bake for 7 minutes in a moderate oven. When cool, spread with whipped cream, roll up and dust with sugar.

Pignoli-Kipferln
Crescent-Shaped Nut Biscuits

Ingredients:
200 g. almonds
200 g. sugar
4 egg whites
1 teaspoon vanilla-flavoured sugar
grated lemon peel
60 g. pine kernels

Method:
Blanch and grind the almonds, mix with the sugar and stiffly beaten egg white, add some grated lemon peel and cook this mixture over a gentle heat until it is soft. Then spread the pine kernels over the working surface and roll small strips of the almond mixture in this, shaping them into crescents. Place the biscuits on a greased baking tray and bake in a low oven. Glaze with spun sugar whilst still hot.

Meraner Traubenstrudel
Grape Strudel

Ingredients:
For the pastry:
250 g. flour
1 egg
2 dessertspoons oil
pinch of salt
a little (approx. $\frac{1}{16}$ l.) water

For the filling:
1 kg. grapes
100 g. sugar
100 g. breadcrumbs
lemon peel
1 teaspoon powdered cinnamon
50 g. melted butter

Method:
Prepare a classic strudel pastry: mix the flour, egg, salt and oil to a smooth paste, carefully adding the lukewarm water mixed with a little vinegar. Shape the pastry into a ball, brush with oil and leave to rest for half an hour. Then roll out on a floured cloth and, palms downwards, pull the pastry outwards from the centre until it is paper thin, but without it tearing.
Sprinkle the breadcrumbs over the pastry, distribute the grapes and the sugar (with the cinnamon and lemon peel) over the breadcrumbs and carefully roll up the pastry as tightly as possible, by pulling the cloth. Brush the strudel with the melted butter and bake in a preheated oven for 30 to 40 minutes at approx. 200° C. Dust with icing sugar whilst still hot.

Chopped or ground nuts or pine kernels can also be added to the filling.

Apple strudel and **cherry strudel** are popular in the Tyrol and throughout the whole of Austria; they are prepared with the same pastry and in the same way.

Maronitorte
Chestnut Gateau

Ingredients:
280 g. sugar
12 egg yolks
12 stiffly beaten egg whites
140 g. chocolate
100 g. chestnuts

Method:
Beat one third of the sugar with the egg yolks until fluffy, add the melted chocolate. Shell and skin the chestnuts and rub through a sieve. Beat the remaining sugar with the 12 egg whites and carefully fold this into the egg yolk mixture alternately with the chestnuts. Bake for 1 hour at 180° C, leave to cool, cut through the middle and sandwich with the following filling.

Filling:
Blend 100 g sieved chestnuts and 50 g. sugar with ½ l. stiffly whipped cream and fill the cake with this, using the remainder to cover the cake and decorating with marrons glacés or with chocolate-coated chestnuts.

Tiroler Kletzenbrot
Tyrolean Fruit Loaf

Ingredients:
2 kg. well-risen white or brown bread dough (from the baker)
1 kg. dried pears
1 kg. damsons
½ kg. figs
250 g. raisins
200 g. nuts
5 g. cinnamon
5 g. mixed spice
5 g. powdered cloves
5 dessertspoons rum

Method:
Stew the dried pears, stone the damsons and cut these and the figs into small strips. Add the coarsely chopped nuts, the spices and the rum. Mix well and leave to stand for several hours. If not moist enough, add a little of the water from the pears. Knead the fruit mixture with 1½ kg. bread dough from the baker. Roll out the remaining ½ kg. and wrap it around the fruit dough, having shaped this into an oblong. Cover and leave in a warm place to rise. This takes about 4 hours. Brush with water and bake in a slow oven for 2 hours. Brush with sugar water and place in the oven again briefly. Cool and keep for at least one week before using. This fruit bread will keep fresh for several months.

Notes and Further Recipes

Notes and Further Recipes

Notes and Further Recipes

Notes and Further Recipes

Notes and Further Recipes

Notes and Further Recipes